Fossil Fuels: Preferred

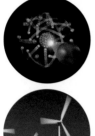

Nuclear Energy: The Future Is Now

Renewable Energy: Endless Power

THREE PERSUASIVE ESSAYS
ABOUT ENERGY SOURCES FOR THE 21ST CENTURY

by Katherine Follett

Table of Contents

Persuasive Essays

What is a persuasive essay?

A persuasive essay is an essay that tries to convince readers to believe or do something. A persuasive essay has a strong point of view about an idea or a problem. It includes facts and examples to support an opinion, and it usually suggests a solution.

What is the purpose of a persuasive essay?

People write persuasive essays to sway, or change the minds of, their readers. The writer wants readers to see his or her point of view and take action. This attempt to persuade readers is sometimes called an argument. The writer may also need to take into account an opposing viewpoint and give reasons why it is flawed. This is called a counterargument.

Who is the audience for a persuasive essay?

People write persuasive essays to all kinds of people: parents, friends, citizens, business leaders, world leaders, and others. For example, someone might write to a leader about a law they don't agree with. The writer might want to persuade the leader to change the law.

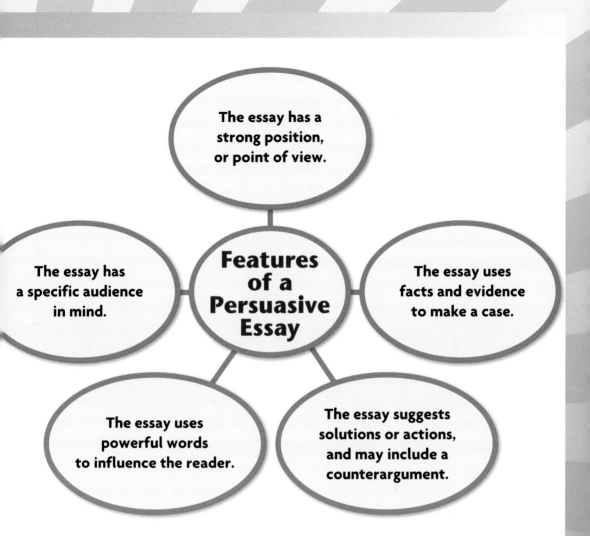

The essay has a strong position, or point of view.

The essay has a specific audience in mind.

Features of a Persuasive Essay

The essay uses facts and evidence to make a case.

The essay uses powerful words to influence the reader.

The essay suggests solutions or actions, and may include a counterargument.

How do you read a persuasive essay?

Keep in mind that the writer wants you to support his or her position. Ask yourself, *What is this writer's position, or opinion? Does he or she support it with facts and good reasons? Do I agree?* A good persuasive writer knows his or her audience. The writer knows what facts and reasons might change the reader's mind.

Tools for Readers and Writers

State and Defend Your Position

Writers of persuasive essays have strong opinions, or beliefs, which they must make very clear to the reader. Then they need to convince their readers to have the same opinions. To do this, they support their position with factual information (that can be proven). They give concrete examples of why the position must be taken seriously. Writers often use language to get readers to share their emotions about the issue.

Suffixes

Good writers use as few words as possible to convey meaning. One way they accomplish this task is by using suffixes. When suffixes are placed at the end of a root or base word, the meaning of that root word changes. For example, the suffix **-y** means "being or having." Instead of saying "being like fruit," authors say **fruity**. Instead of saying "having sun," writers say **sunny**.

Text Structure and Organization

Writers put words together in several ways called text structures or patterns. These text structures include cause and effect, problem and solution, compare and contrast, steps in a process or sequence, and descriptions. In many cases, writers use key words and phrases that help readers determine the text structure being used. Other times, the reader has to think about the text's structure. Knowing how the writer organized the text can help readers better understand and remember what they've read.

Famous Persuasive Essays

A persuasive essay provides a writer with an opportunity to share thoughts on a topic he or she is knowledgeable and passionate about. The writer wants to first inspire the reader to think. Then the writer hopes the essay will help the reader solidify his current thinking on the topic or change his thinking around to the writer's point of view.

Persuasive essays on thousands of topics have been written over the centuries. Topics range from war to capital punishment to spaying/neutering pets to what type of energy we should be using to power our planet. Here are just a few examples of famous essays that made people think—and often changed their thinking.

Common Sense

From the time "Common Sense" was first published in 1776, it instantly became the most influential essay ever written about the American colonies' need for independence from Great Britain. Written by Thomas Paine but published anonymously, the essay states that, "The cause of America is, in a great measure, the cause of all mankind." Using powerful language and facts to support his point of view, Paine laid out a logical argument for independence. Historians believe this essay, written at the early stages of the American Revolution, inspired colonists and deepened the determination of those already committed to the cause.

Self-Reliance

First published in 1841, this essay was American writer Ralph Waldo Emerson's strongest argument against conformity. One of Emerson's major themes as a writer was to urge people to think for themselves. This essay contains many powerful passages, including the now famous quote: "A foolish consistency is the hobgoblin of little minds."

Emerson's essay strongly influenced many people at the time, including his friend and fellow author Henry David Thoreau.

The Federalist Papers

This group of eighty-five essays published between 1787 and 1788 was written to persuade voters in New York State to ratify the proposed U.S. Constitution. Published in several New York newspapers and written by a variety of writers, including Alexander Hamilton, James Madison, and John Jay, the Federalist Papers explained how the new government would work and urged people to adopt the Constitution. Writing in the first essay, Hamilton said, "I am convinced that this is the safest course for your liberty, your dignity, and your happiness." While it is not clear how much the Federalist Papers influenced New Yorkers, the U.S. Constitution was indeed ratified in 1788.

On Civil Disobedience

Writer Henry David Thoreau wrote this essay urging people to follow their consciences in pursuit of what they believed is right even if it meant going against the government (but in a nonviolent way). He encouraged people to decline to participate in unjust laws. The oft-heard quote "That government is best which governs least" was written by Thoreau in this essay. Not only did "On Civil Disobedience" influence people in Thoreau's day, but it has been said to have influenced future peaceful leaders, including Mohandas Gandhi and Martin Luther King Jr.

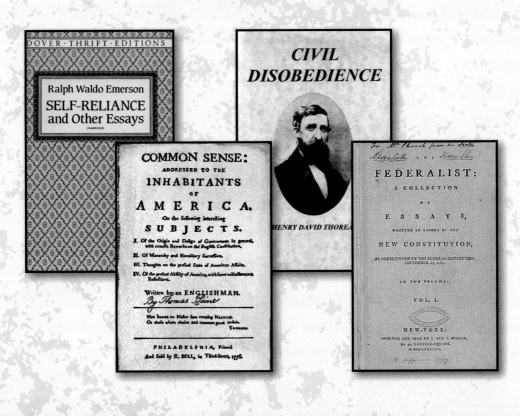

Fossil Fuels: America's Preferred Power

From the moment you hear your alarm buzz in the morning to the second you turn off your light at night, you—along with billions of people around the world—rely on fossil fuels. Coal makes the electricity you depend on; oil powers the car, truck, bus, plane, or train that takes you to where you need to go; and natural gas warms your room and cooks your food when you come home. Fossil fuels are America's best source of power. The energy they provide is on demand continuously. Fossil fuels are astonishingly diverse, doing more tasks than any other source of power. On top of all that, they are by far the most affordable source of energy on the planet.

Power for Every Minute

America's cities, factories, highways, and hospitals run twenty-four hours a day, seven days a week. Only an on-demand source of power such as fossil fuels can provide the **continuous**, around-the-clock electricity we need. Our lights, appliances, and machines use electric current, which is a constantly moving stream of electricity. It is notoriously hard to store electricity—even the best batteries last only a few hours. Wind power, solar power, and water power are practical in only a few places, and they can fade in and out depending on the weather—stranding our homes and hospitals without vital electricity. On the other hand, fossil fuels are storable, portable, and available wherever and whenever we need power. Only fossil fuels can meet our worldwide, constant, ever-changing need for electricity.

Power for Every Purpose

We don't rely on fossil fuels for just electricity—the unsurpassed variety of fossil fuels meets every one of America's many energy needs. Gasoline and diesel, made from oil, run our cars, trucks, trains, and farm equipment. Jet fuel comes from oil, too. Natural gas warms our homes, heats our water, and cooks our food. Fossil fuels can handle all these jobs because they are wonderfully easy to control, transport, change, and burn. By contrast, solar, wind, water, and nuclear power make only electricity—which leaves our entire transportation system stuck! There is just no other energy source with as many practical uses as fossil fuels.

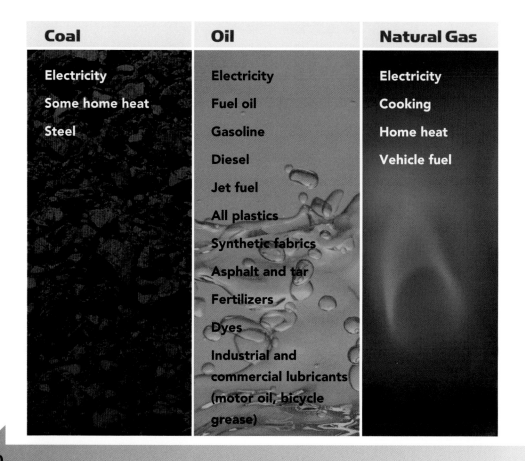

Coal	Oil	Natural Gas
Electricity	Electricity	Electricity
Some home heat	Fuel oil	Cooking
Steel	Gasoline	Home heat
	Diesel	Vehicle fuel
	Jet fuel	
	All plastics	
	Synthetic fabrics	
	Asphalt and tar	
	Fertilizers	
	Dyes	
	Industrial and commercial lubricants (motor oil, bicycle grease)	

Power for Pennies

The most compelling reason to use fossil fuels is their unbelievably low cost. A single kilowatt-hour of electricity from coal costs as little as five cents. Electricity from wind currently costs about twice as much, and solar electricity costs over five times as much! Without inexpensive energy from fossil fuels, many people would literally be left in the cold, unable to afford to keep their families warm. Businesses would have to spend more to keep their factories, offices, and trucks running, which would raise the price of everything you buy and use each day. Our entire economy depends on the reliably affordable power of fossil fuels.

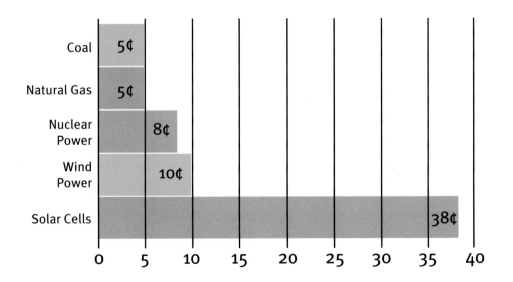

Power for the Planet

Recently, some groups have criticized fossil fuels, saying that the way Americans use energy causes **environmental** problems such as air pollution and climate change. They claim that **renewable** resources or nuclear power would be more environmentally friendly than fossil fuels. But the truth is that every source of energy has some environmental problems: solar cells are manufactured with toxic heavy metals; wind turbines kill birds and cause noise **pollution**; and hydropower dams drown rivers and everything that depends on them, from endangered amphibians to ocean fish that can no longer swim upstream to spawn. On the other hand, cutting-edge technologies make fossil fuels clean and safe. Clean-coal technology takes impurities out of raw coal long before they ever get to the power plant, and scrubbing smokestacks remove the remaining **pollutants** before

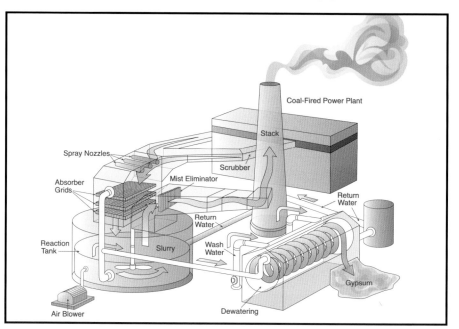

This diagram shows how current technology has helped coal clean up its act.

they ever leave. And though it is true that burning fossil fuels releases a greenhouse gas called carbon dioxide, we now have carbon-capture technologies that trap this gas before it enters the atmosphere. The carbon dioxide is injected deep underground, sometimes into the very wells or mines where we first got the fossil fuels! Technology makes it possible to enjoy the enormous advantages of fossil fuels while still protecting our environment.

This new scrubbing smokestack at a coal-fired power plant can reduce sulfur dioxide emissions by ninety-five percent.

Fossil fuels have been the world's go-to energy source for more than 100 years, and billions of people rely on them every day. They make energy steadily, predictably, and on demand. They have an astonishing array of uses, powering not just our lights and appliances, but also the vehicles on our roads and the planes in the air. And their cost simply can't be beat, making power affordable for everyone. Fossil fuels make our rich and convenient way of life possible, and cutting-edge technologies make sure they will be environmentally sustainable for decades to come. It makes sense that we use fossil fuels more than any other source of energy—they are the best source of power on the planet.

Reread the Persuasive Essay

Understand the Essay
- What is this persuasive essay about?
- What side is the author on?
- The author provides arguments that support her claim. Identify two.
- The author discusses counterarguments against her claim. Identify two.
- How does the essay end?

Focus on Comprehension:
Text Structure and Organization
- Identify two examples of compare-and-contrast key words and phrases that indicate the author has used that text structure to organize this essay.
- Reread "Power for Pennies." The author uses a multiple cause-and-effect text structure in this section without using key words. Identify the cause-and-effect relationship.
- Which text structure does the author use in the final paragraph?

Analyze the Tools Writers Use:
State and Defend Your Position
- What position does the author take in her essay?
- What facts and examples does the author give to support her position?
- What emotion words does the author use to share her opinion?

Text Structure	Key Words		
Cause and Effect/ Problem and Solution	• so • because	• therefore • as a result	• consequently
Compare and Contrast	• however • but	• too • instead	• on the other hand
Sequence of Events/ Steps in a Process	• first • after • then	• now • later • finally	• not long after
Description	• also • in fact • details	• for instance • sense words	

Focus on Words: Suffixes

Make a chart like the one below. For each word, identify its part of speech. Then identify the base or root word and suffix. Finally, identify the word's meaning.

Page	Word	Part of Speech	Base or Root Word	Suffix	Definition
9	continuous				
12	environmental				
12	renewable				
12	pollution				
12	pollutants				

Nuclear Energy: The Future Is Now

L et's say you get to decide, once and for all, how America makes its electricity. How will you choose? Fossil fuels are cheap and they provide continuous power wherever and whenever we need it, but they are terrible for the environment and they will soon run out. Renewable resources last forever and are safe for the planet, but they cost far more than fossil fuels and can fade in and out depending on the weather, disrupting our critical power supply. Wouldn't it be great if you could combine the advantages of fossil fuels and renewable energy, while eliminating their disadvantages? It turns out that one source of power does just that. That source is nuclear energy, which creates electricity using the enormous power of nuclear reactions. It is by far the best choice to fill America's energy needs. Nuclear energy makes energy on demand, it does not release air pollution or greenhouse gases, it is **inexpensive**, it is safe, and it will last as long as we need power.

Nuclear Is On-Demand

There's no question about one thing: we must have steady, on-demand electricity so our hospitals, military, police, firefighters, and other vital safety and security systems can run continuously—not to mention our homes, schools, and businesses. Nuclear energy provides the most stable and steady energy in the world. Nuclear power plants operate every minute of every day, no matter the weather, and we can build them anywhere power is needed. The supply of nuclear fuel, or uranium, is also large, safe, and stable. The International Atomic Energy Agency estimates we have enough uranium to power the world's nuclear reactors for 2,500 years! Nuclear power is steady and on-demand now, and it will stay steady and on-demand far into the future.

Nuclear Is Clean

Nuclear energy has another huge advantage over today's more common energy sources: it emits no smelly air pollution or dangerous greenhouse gases. Nuclear power **generators** give off only pure steam or warm, clean water while they generate electricity. They don't create carbon dioxide that contributes to acid rain and global warming. The solid waste from a nuclear power plant is kept isolated in completely sealed concrete or steel tanks, so it never comes in contact with people, plants, animals, or soil. The U.S. government's Nuclear Regulatory Commission gives our nuclear power plants glowing environmental reports.

Nuclear Is Low-Cost

One of the biggest factors you must consider as you choose a source of energy is cost. Nuclear plants already in operation make electricity for far less than wind or solar power. Nuclear energy can even cost as little as fossil fuels, our "cheapest" source of energy. Cheapest is in quotes because there are hidden costs to fossil fuels, beyond the cost to the environment. The price of importing fossil fuels is rapidly rising as our natural supplies dwindle and we must mine deeper, drill deeper, and compete with other nations to get them. But we have enough uranium, the main ingredient for nuclear fuel, to keep the price low for thousands of years.

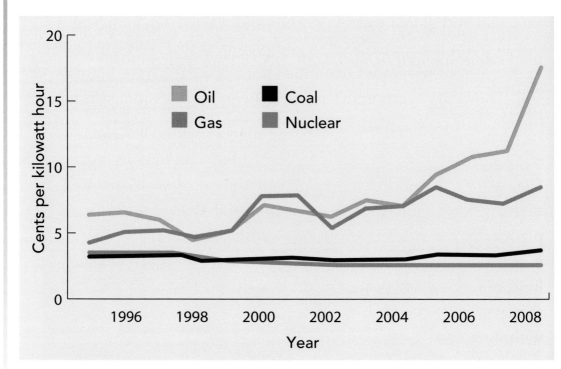

Nuclear energy is as cheap as fossil fuels, but because the fuel supply is steady, the price does not fluctuate.

Nuclear power plants have safety measures at every step of the process.

Nuclear Is Safe

Nuclear energy has clear advantages over every other source of energy, yet the United States hasn't built a new nuclear power plant since 1978, even as our demand for energy has grown. In the past few decades, many groups have spread fear about the safety of nuclear power. But a look at the evidence will show that these fears are baseless. From the design of a plant to employee training to public reports, safety is and always has been the nuclear industry's top priority. Contrary to misconceptions, nuclear power plants do not—I repeat, do not—release dangerous levels of radiation. In fact, workers at nuclear power plants are exposed to less radiation than airplane pilots get from **natural** cosmic rays! A nuclear power plant cannot cause a nuclear-bomb-type explosion; the nuclear fuel is spread out in a way that makes it physically impossible for this kind of runaway reaction. Modern nuclear fuels will simply stop reacting in the rare case of a problem—they shut down naturally, without a human or even a machine intervening, preventing nuclear accidents. Radioactive nuclear waste is always kept isolated in air-tight, leak-proof containers so it has no chance of harming people or the environment.

Some nations even recycle nuclear waste, helping to cut down on radioactive waste and giving us an even bigger supply of nuclear fuel. Compared to other energy sources—which experience routine accidents during mining, shipping, and burning fuel, not to mention the terrible health effects of air pollution—nuclear energy has a top-notch safety record.

Nuclear energy combines the best features of every other energy source. It has the practicality and flexibility of fossil fuels but without the pollution or the threat of running out. It has the enormous, sustainable, and nearly infinite power of renewable resources, without the problems of **unpredictability** and limited locations. It has the environmental friendliness of "green" sources such as solar or wind power, without the high price. It is also one of the safest industries in the world. Other **technologically** advanced nations such as France and Japan have gone nuclear. Nuclear energy is the best source of energy for the future of America, too. It's time to make the future happen now.

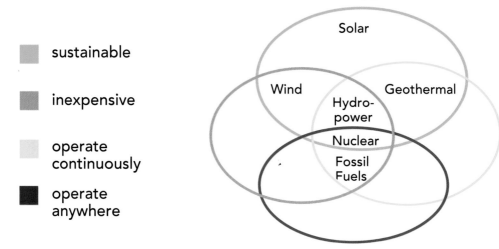

sustainable

inexpensive

operate continuously

operate anywhere

Nuclear energy combines the best features of all energy sources.

Understand the Essay
- What is this persuasive essay about?
- What side is the author on?
- The author provides arguments that support her claim. Identify three.
- The author discusses counterarguments against her claim. Identify two.
- How does the essay end?

Focus on Comprehension:
Text Structure and Organization
- The main text structure for this essay is description. Identify three parts of the text where description is used.
- Reread "Nuclear Is Safe." The author uses the cause-and-effect key word **so** in this section. Locate the word **so** and identify the cause-and-effect relationship connected with it.
- What compare-and-contrast word does the author use in "Nuclear Is Safe"?

Analyze the Tools Writers Use:
State and Defend Your Position
- What position does the author take in her essay?
- What facts and examples does the author give to support her position?
- What emotion words does the author use to share her opinion?

Focus on Words: Suffixes
Make a chart like the one below. For each word, identify its part of speech. Then identify the base or root word and suffix. Finally, identify the word's meaning.

Page	Word	Part of Speech	Base or Root Word	Suffix	Definition
16	inexpensive				
17	generators				
19	natural				
20	unpredictability				
20	technologically				

Renewable Energy: Endless Power

Imagine discovering the perfect source of electricity. This **miraculous** power source will never run out. It can be found absolutely anywhere on the planet, so people can make electricity in their own backyards. On top of all that, this ideal power source doesn't release pollution or greenhouse gases. Well, that power source isn't imaginary! It's called renewable energy, and there is not one, but three major kinds. Solar power taps into the endless power of sunlight. Wind power harnesses the force of the wind. Hydropower brings us steady, clean energy from flowing water. Solar, wind, and water power are our best sources of energy for making electricity, because each is totally **limitless**, widely available, and environmentally safe.

The writer begins with a strong statement in favor of renewable energy.

The writer concludes the introduction with three themes she will address in the essay.

The writer presents renewability as evidence of the superiority of solar, wind, and water power over other types of energy.

Limitless Power

One of the biggest advantages of renewable energy is right in its name: it's renewable, meaning it doesn't get used up, no matter how much power we use. Most other energy resources, including nuclear power and fossil fuels, are nonrenewable. Once we take energy from nuclear fuel or burn coal, oil, or natural gas, those fuels are used up forever. But sunlight, wind, and flowing water aren't destroyed or burned up as we use them. They provide more energy than we could ever need, as long as the sun shines, the wind blows, and water flows downhill.

Solar power will last as long as the sun shines—about another five billion years!

Local Power

Another appealing attribute of renewable resources is how common and widely available they are. Every place where people live has sun, wind, or water nearby. Solar cells, flat panels that convert sunlight into electricity, can go anywhere the sun shines, turning schools, homes, offices, even parking lots into private power plants. Hydropower already provides one-fifth of America's electricity, and the U.S. Department of Energy has found over 5,000 places where we could build new hydropower stations on local rivers across the nation. Wind power is just as convenient. Thousands of homeowners have installed graceful wind turbines on their properties, making their own electricity each time a breeze blows.

Private wind turbines create so much electricity that people often sell electricity back to the power company. Imagine making money instead of paying high home-heating bills!

Keeping our energy sources close to home has advantages besides saving money.

The fact that renewable sources of energy are easily accessible is further evidence of its advantages. The writer also presents facts about how much this type of energy is already in use.

The writer uses the adjective **graceful** to describe wind turbines, hoping this positive image will sway readers to her position.

Fossil fuels and uranium, the fuel for nuclear power, are found only in certain parts of the world, and many of those places are outside the United States. Today, we spend billions of dollars on fossil fuels, especially oil. This supports dangerous **dictators** and nations that wish us harm. Switching to local renewable resources is a smart move for our national safety.

When describing other energy sources, the writer also uses powerful negative terms such as "dangerous dictators" and "national safety" in order to influence readers.

Clean Power

No matter how you look at it, renewable energy is the most environmentally friendly source of power, especially compared to fossil fuels and nuclear energy. Coal mining has literally torn apart entire mountains in the Appalachians, demolishing the community of plants and animals that lives there. Drilling and shipping oil frequently leads to spills—such as the catastrophic oil-drilling accident in the Gulf of Mexico in May 2010—that threaten not only

The writer continues to build the argument for renewable energy by presenting the environmental disadvantages to fossil fuels and nuclear energy.

wildlife, but also the fishing industry that depends on healthy seas, **tourism**, and other local economies. Nuclear energy creates deadly, cancer-causing, radioactive waste and we haven't found a place to store it safely. So it simply piles up at the nuclear power plants. Coal, oil, and natural gas release air pollution and carbon dioxide, which warms our climate. A warmer climate endangers wildlife such as polar bears; causes storms, droughts, and wildfires; and raises sea levels, flooding populated coastal areas.

Strip-mining of coal has destroyed many places in West Virginia.

Solar, wind, and water power are free of these problems. Renewable resources create electricity without releasing air pollution or toxic wastes that harm human, plant, or animal health. They do not add greenhouse gases to the atmosphere or change our climate. For the sake of the world's plants and animals—and for ourselves—renewable resources are the best choice.

Practical Power

The writer presents an argument against renewable resources and then uses facts and evidence to make a counterargument that refutes it.

Not everyone is convinced that renewable resources are the way to go, even with all of these clear advantages. What happens, they ask, if the wind stops blowing or the sun goes down? These critics only consider conditions in one small area at any one time. In reality, the sun and wind never stop across the entire country at once, or even across an entire region, and our vast grid of electrical wires moves energy from where it's made to where it's needed at any moment. While the sun is down in the evening in New York, it still shines brightly on solar cells in California. While the wind might momentarily ease in one area, it generates power steadily on nearby mountain ranges, prairies, or coastlines. These critics also ignore hydropower, which runs 24 hours a day, 7 days a week, 365 days a year. In fact, the truly **impractical** energy source is fossil fuels.

In the 1970s, some oil-producing countries suddenly decided to stop selling oil to the United States. Energy prices skyrocketed, and many areas of the country simply ran out of fuel. That could happen again at any moment. And because fossil fuels and nuclear fuel are nonrenewable, someday they will run out forever. On the other hand, if we build more solar cells, wind turbines, and hydropower stations, we'll capture sunlight, wind, and water over even larger areas, ensuring a more continuous supply of electricity. The more renewable energy we use, the more plentiful it becomes!

Long lines of cars outside gas stations were not an unusual sight during the Oil Embargo of the 1970s.

Renewable resources provide everything Americans need from an energy source. We need energy that is plentiful now and won't run out as we power our future.

We need energy that is easy to get, local, and safe for our nation. And the whole world needs a stable climate and healthy forests, croplands, coasts, and wild places. Only renewable resources give us limitless, convenient, local, safe energy while preserving the environment on which we all depend. There is no need to imagine a perfect source of power—renewable resources are already here. We need to increase our usage of renewable energy and decrease our reliance on fossil fuels and nuclear energy.

The writer concludes by summarizing the essay's main points in favor of renewable energy, using an upbeat tone that encourages people to use it, and suggests a course of action.

Understand the Essay
- What is this persuasive essay about?
- What side is the author on?
- The author provides arguments that support her claim. Identify three.
- The author discusses counterarguments against her claim. Identify two.
- How does the essay end?

Focus on Comprehension:
Text Structure and Organization
- Reread the last sentence in the first paragraph. What text structure does the author use?
- Reread "Clean Power." The author uses description and compare-and-contrast text structures. Explain how.
- Reread "Practical Power." The author uses cause-and-effect and compare-and-contrast text structures. Explain how.

Analyze the Tools Writers Use:
State and Defend Your Position
- What position does the author take in her essay?
- What facts and examples does the author give to support her position?
- What emotion words does the author use to share her opinion?

Focus on Catchy Titles
Authors include strong leads, or hooks, in persuasive essays. But what about titles? Titles are just as important, if not more so, than strong leads because they catch the reader's eye before the lead. That is why good titles are referred to as catchy titles. Reread the titles used in this book. What about the titles caught your attention? What did you think the articles were going to be about?

Focus on Words: Suffixes

Make a chart like the one below. For each word, identify its part of speech. Then identify the base or root word and suffix. Finally, identify the word's meaning.

Page	Word	Part of Speech	Base or Root Word	Suffix	Definition
22	miraculous				
22	limitless				
24	dictators				
25	tourism				
26	impractical				

America's large and efficient electrical grid allows us to transfer power from where it is made to where it is needed.

How does an author write a
PERSUASIVE ESSAY?

Reread "Renewable Energy: Endless Power" and think about what Katherine Follett did to write it. How did she state her position? How did she support it effectively? How did she end the essay?

1. Choose a Problem to Write About

Remember, the writer needs to state a position for or against something. The writer may want to talk about a problem that needs solving or to either support or defend a cause. For instance, the writer argues that renewable sources of energy are the perfect energy source because they are clean, available locally, and limitless.

2. Identify Your Audience

The audience is whom you are writing to, the person or people you need to convince. Writers must present facts and reasons that will convince their audience. The writer of this essay was writing to those who primarily rely on fossil fuels for energy, as well as to those who think that nuclear energy is a good idea.

3. Provide Facts, Examples, and Values to Support and Clarify Your Position

Writers of persuasive essays support their position by:
- providing factual information (information that can be proven)
- providing concrete, real-world examples (things they have done, heard, or seen)
- clarifying the relevant values for your audience (providing perspective)
- presenting the facts, examples, and values in an order that helps build a strong argument

4. Provide a Solution or Suggest an Action

A writer may provide one or more solutions to a problem or present a specific call to action. In this essay, the writer suggests a decreased reliance on fossil fuels and nuclear energy and an increased usage of renewable sources of energy.

5. Write a Strong Conclusion

As a writer, you should summarize your argument in your conclusion and refer to the first paragraph or opening statement and the main points you made throughout the essay. Ask yourself, *Is the conclusion a logical outcome of the arguments presented in the essay?*

Problem	The writer wants people to understand that renewable sources of energy are our best energy choices for the present day and into the future.
Audience	everyone who currently relies primarily on fossil fuels for energy, as well as those who think nuclear energy is the best energy source
Supporting Facts and Examples	• Renewable energy is readily available; it can be found anywhere on the planet. • Renewable energy doesn't release pollution or greenhouse gases into the environment. • Renewable energy is limitless: We will never run out of water, wind, or solar power.
Solution to the Problem	• Renewable energy is the practical choice. For example, we can store solar energy so we have it when we need it. • People should decrease reliance on fossil fuels and nuclear energy and increase use of renewable energy.

Glossary

continuous   (kun-TIN-yoo-us) uninterrupted (page 9)

dictators   (DIK-tay-terz) leaders with total power (page 24)

environmental   (in-vy-run-MEN-tul) having to do with the environment (page 12)

generators   (JEH-nuh-ray-terz) engines that change mechanical energy into electrical energy (page 17)

impractical   (im-PRAK-tih-kul) not practical or sensible (page 26)

inexpensive   (ih-nik-SPEN-siv) reasonable in price (page 16)

limitless   (LIH-mit-les) having no maximum quantity (page 22)

miraculous   (muh-RA-kyuh-lus) marvelous (page 22)

natural   (NA-chuh-rul) existing in nature (page 19)

pollutants   (puh-LOO-tunts)things that pollute (page 12)

pollution   (puh-LOO-shun) anything that makes the environment dirty (page 12)

renewable   (rih-NOO-uh-bul) capable of being renewed (page 12)

technologically   (tek-nuh-LAH-jih-klee) in a technological way (page 20)

tourism   (TOR-ih-zum) an industry that provides goods and services to people who travel for pleasure (page 25)

unpredictability   (un-prih-dik-tuh-BIH-lih-tee) the state of being difficult or impossible to predict or know in advance (page 20)